GROUNDCOVER
SERIES

Text research: Bernadette Sheehan

Acknowledgements

I thank Caroline Jarrold and Malcolm Crampton for giving me this commission, Bernadette Sheehan for the difficult task of researching the text, the editorial team of Sarah Letts and Geoffrey Sutton for their patience as photographic deadlines crept nearer and Peter Salt for his valuable assistance. Thanks also to Kaarin Wall for adding the creative flair, who with the editorial team, did an excellent job of pulling it all together.

I also thank Neil Jinkerson and John Brooks for their generous advice and, finally, Sarah for whose motivation and encouragement I shall be ever grateful.

Andrew Perkins

The photographer and publisher acknowledge with thanks the assistance of Norwich City Council and the many other people, institutions and companies who have made this book possible.

Front cover picture: Elm Hill at night
Back cover picture: Bishop Bridge

Designed and produced by
Jarrold Publishing,
Whitefriars, Norwich NR3 1TR

All photographs by
© Andrew Perkins

© Jarrold Publishing 2001

ISBN 0-7117-1609-9

Printed in Belgium.

1/01

PUBLISHER'S NOTE
Variant and archaic spellings have been retained in quoted material, while the modern spellings of place-names have been used in headings.

The inclusion of a photograph in this book does not necessarily imply public access to the building illustrated.

Norwich

ANDREW PERKINS

JARROLD
publishing

A boss in Norwich Cathedral cloisters depicting the baptism of Christ

GROUNDCOVER
SERIES

NORWICH

Norwich School of Art and Design interior, St George's Street

Contents

Pageantry at the Lord Mayor's Procession

Introduction

'Norwich is (as you please) either a City in an Orchard, or an Orchard in a City, so equally are Houses and Trees blended in it … the inhabitants participate nothing of the rusticalness of the one, but altogether of the urbanity and civility of the other,' wrote Thomas Fuller in 1662, and his description of the city still rings true. Although a fast-growing regional centre, Norwich has lost surprisingly little of the character that Fuller found so appealing. You only have to take a stroll through the Cathedral Close or along the riverside walk to experience an

'orchard' in the middle of the city. Ancient Mousehold Heath, its 150 acres (61 ha) of wild heathland a vivid counterpoint to Norwich's unique collection of 1930s city parks, offers another peaceful retreat from twenty-first-century bustle. Even the contemporary Castle Mall shopping centre is topped with a 4-acre (1.6-ha) oasis of greenery and water features.

The city's 'urbanity and civility' are equally evident. The Normans left as their legacy the magnificent cathedral and castle, while exquisite buildings such as the Assembly House and Octagon Chapel date from

Norwich's prosperous Georgian era. And, dotted throughout the city, which boasts the most complete medieval street pattern in England, stand more pre-Reformation churches than any other city in Europe, mostly made of local flint and demonstrating the great skill of the medieval builders.

The word 'Norwich' derives from the Anglo-Saxon *Norðwic*. From this small settlement on the River Wensum, Norwich grew to become the largest provincial city in England in the seventeenth century, and for 500 years, until the Industrial Revolution, it was

the main centre of worsted manufacture in the country. Many other manufacturing industries flourished in the nineteenth century. Today the Riverside leisure complex is the latest commercial development on the river's banks.

Careful to preserve its unique heritage, Norwich also looks confidently to the future. It is still very much the 'fine city' that George Borrow so admired in the nineteenth century, as the following pages reveal.

ANDREW PERKINS

THE ASSEMBLY HOUSE

The eye then commands a suit of rooms of 143 feet illuminated by ten branches holding 150 candles; and the company forming into one row may dance the whole length of the building, and then is presented such a scene of beauty and splendour as has few equals. The principal assembly is in the October sessions week.

R. BEATNIFFE
The Norfolk Tour or Traveller's Pocket-Companion
1773

Norwich can be proud of its Assembly House. No other town of its size in England has anything like it.

NIKOLAUS PEVSNER AND BILL WILSON
The Buildings of England: Norfolk 1, Norwich and North-East
1962

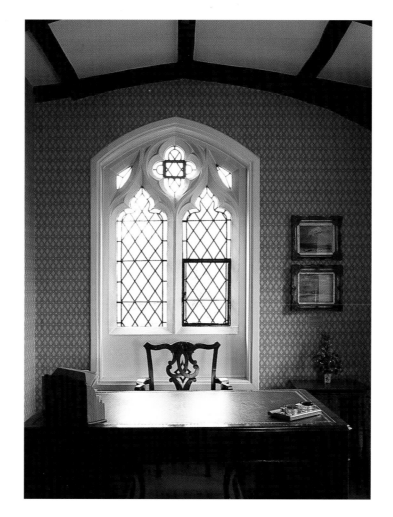

GUILDHALL

Whoso have any quarrel
   or plea,
If in the Gildhall at Norwich
   it be;
Be it false be it true,
If he but withstand John Hawke
   John Querdling
Nicholas Waleys
   John Belaugh John Mey
Sore shall him rue,
For they'll rule all the court
   with their laws new.

Rhyme of 1433, quoted in
People of Medieval Norwich
by Charles B. Jewson

Norwich occupies a unique place in the history of libraries: it has the distinction of having established in 1608 one of the earliest provincial libraries, if not the first in England, and it was the first municipality to adopt the Public Library Act, 1850.

GEORGE A. STEPHEN (CITY LIBRARIAN)
Three Centuries of a City Library
1917

THE FORUM

The Forum, incorporating the new Norfolk and Norwich Millennium Library and the USAAF 2nd Air Division Memorial Library, opened in autumn 2001. As well as library facilities, the three-storey complex includes a multimedia exploration of the history of the area, training facilities, visitor information, café, restaurant, exhibitions and entertainment in the atrium. From 2002, local BBC radio and television programmes will be broadcast from the site.

CITY HALL

The City Hall … must go down in history as the foremost English public building of between the wars. It lies in an enviable position, raised above the spacious Market Place, and makes the best of that position. Its tower, 185 ft high, is a beacon, and it is successfully contrasted against the stretching front with its slender portico.

Nikolaus Pevsner and Bill Wilson
The Buildings of England: Norfolk 1, Norwich and North-East
1962

Opened by George VI in 1938, City Hall has a bold Scandinavian design that also shows the influence of Egyptian styles popular after the discovery of Tutankhamun's tomb. It was originally orange in colour, and referred to locally as 'marmalade hall'.

City Hall

The Council Chamber at City Hall is panelled in Honduras and Cuban mahogany. Many of the building's original decorations and fittings have been carefully preserved.

THE MARKET PLACE

A broad space called the Hay market [is] on a hill a very steep descent all well pitch'd as before, this comes to another space for a market to sell hoggs in; one runs along behind, which is all for stalls for the Country butchers that bring their meate for the supply of the town … there is a very large Market place and Hall and Cross for fruite and little things every day, and also a place under pillars for the Corn market.

CELIA FIENNES
The Illustrated Journeys of Celia Fiennes
1685–c. 1712

GENTLEMAN'S WALK

Here, Crome! Lor'! you must be off to Raynes, the cook-shop on the Gentlemen's Walk, and take this note from the missus. There ain't enough oyster patties sent, and there's another pot of calf's-foot jelly wanting. Come, stir your stumps…

EMMA MARSHALL
Castle Meadow: a story of Norwich a hundred years ago
1899

JARROLDS DEPARTMENT STORE

Jarrolds' select library – subscriptions from 10/6 per Annum, and includes the free use to an entire family of a well-appointed reading room. The library and reading room are approached by an electric lift, heated in cold weather by hot air and kept beautifully cool in summer by electric fans.

Advertisement in *Citizens of No Mean City* (city souvenir)
1910

Jarrolds department store, built from 1903, was designed by George Skipper. The architect had his office above part of the store, and an elaborate terracotta frieze on the side of the building depicts scenes from his life, showing his wife, children and dog overseeing work on a building site.

PUDDING LANE

In respect to food, Norwich people certainly eat less meat than in most industrial centres, and they prefer the home-grown article to foreign or colonial produce. On the other hand, they consume more vegetables, especially potatoes, and flour in the shape of 'pudding'.

C.B. HAWKINS
Norwich – A Social Study
1910

ST PETER MANCROFT

I scarcely remember ever to have seen a more beautiful parish church; the more so because its beauty results not from foreign ornaments, but from the very fine form and structure of it. It is very large, and of uncommon height, and the sides are almost all window … it has a venerable look, and at the same time, surprisingly cheerful.

JOHN WESLEY
Entry dated Sunday, 5 November 1757,
John Wesley's Journal

The world's first-recorded true peal of 5,040 changes took place at St Peter Mancroft in 1715. The east window contains the finest and most extensive collection of the work of the celebrated fifteenth-century school of Norwich glass painters.

COLMAN'S MUSTARD SHOP
THE ROYAL ARCADE

The seed is grown chiefly in Cambridgeshire, Lincolnshire, Essex, Yorkshire and Holland; and by train, wherry and barge it comes in vast quantities to Colman's big storehouses at Carrow and Yarmouth. … There is white seed and brown, and it is a scientific blending of the flour of these two that makes the best condiment. In the Mustard Laboratory, pretty little glass dishes contain the seed in all its 'developments' … and finally the finished mustard in varying and delicate shades of yellow.

Souvenir of a visit to Carrow Works, Norwich
1901

THE ROYAL ARCADE

The Royal Arcade, an art nouveau fantasy by Norwich architect George Skipper, was opened in May 1899 and described at the time as 'a fragment of the Arabian Nights dropped into the heart of the old city'. It features friezes of peacocks, tiled walls and, over the Back of the Inns entrance, a stained glass screen decorated with foliage and white doves.

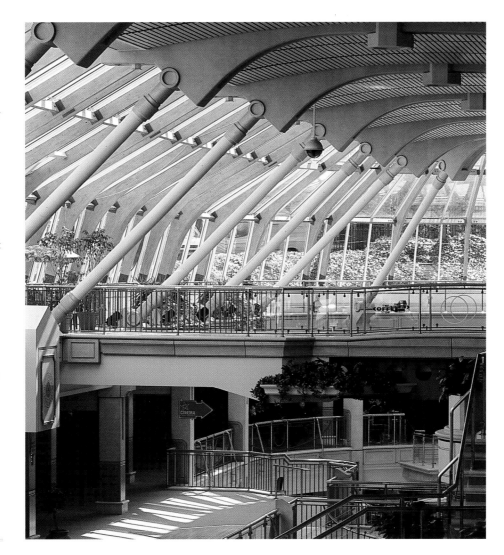

CASTLE MALL

A large part of the million-square-foot Castle Mall development is underground, but natural light flooding through an elegant glass and iron rooflight makes it appear almost weightless.

NORWICH CASTLE

The Castle Museum reopened in 2001 after extensive refurbishment, including a new archaeology gallery featuring Queen Boudica. Other areas, such as the basement of the keep, are now open to the public for the first time, and many galleries have been enhanced or enlarged with a range of interactive, multimedia displays.

NORWICH CASTLE

It has already been hinted that the streets of Norwich are mazy. They are indeed the most perplexing of any town in England. Many roads run into the city, and from every direction. Glancing at the plan of it, these roads resemble the main strands of a spider's web, and the streets the cross webs. In the midst of this maze is the great castle, like the spider himself.

CHARLES G. HARPER
The Norfolk Road: An East Anglian Highway
1901

The ornate Romanesque detail of Norwich Castle's keep dates from the 1830s, when it was refaced, but the decoration remains close to the original, which was unusual in a military building.

TOMBLAND

At the time of the Norman Conquest in 1066, there was a thriving market on Tombland (or 'open space') where a variety of local goods and produce was traded, including North Sea herring, pottery, cloth, and furs from the Continent. The Normans moved the market to its present-day position.

TOMBLAND

They say there are large droves of cattle and flocks of sheep gone up to Castle Hill, and Castle Meadow, and Tombland are full of shows.

EMMA MARSHALL
*Castle Meadow: a story of Norwich
a hundred years ago*
1899

LONDON STREET

Norwich is famed for its churches, but despite appearances, this building in London Street is actually a branch of the National Westminster Bank, dating from 1924.

TOMBLAND

[Norwich] is an antient, large, rich, and populous city: If a stranger was only to ride thro' or view the city of Norwich for a day, he would have … reason to think there was a town without inhabitants … but on the contrary, if he was to view the city, either on a sabbath-day, or any publick occasion, he would wonder where all the people could dwell, the multitude is so great.

DANIEL DEFOE
A Tour through the Whole Island of Great Britain
1724

BRIDEWELL ALLEY

The Bridewell was built by Bartholomew Appleyard about the year 1370. William Appleyard, his son, the first Mayor of Norwich, served his Mayoralty here in 1403. It was purchased by the city in 1585 and used until 1829 as a 'House of Correction' … Its north wall, 79 feet in length and 27 feet in height, is faced with black flints of a very smooth surface so admirably squared and regularly put together, as scarcely to admit the edge of a knife between the joints.

Citizens of No Mean City (city souvenir)
1910

BRIDEWELL MUSEUM

The Bridewell Museum is devoted to local trades and industries, and includes displays on flour-milling, brewing, mustard-producing, chocolate-making, iron-working, manufacture of textiles and boot and shoe-making. There are also examples of early fire appliances, and reconstructions of a smithy and the interior of a pre-war pharmacy.

PRINCES STREET

All their buildings are of an old form, mostly in deep points and much tileing, and their building timber and they playster on laths which they strike out into squares like broad free stone on the outside, which makes their fronts look pretty well.

CELIA FIENNES
The Illustrated Journeys of Celia Fiennes 1685–c. 1712

ST MICHAEL AT PLEA

Medieval Norwich had 57 churches within its city walls, of which 31 still exist, although the majority have been converted for alternative uses. St Michael at Plea, for example, 'so named because the Archdeacon of Norwich holds his pleas or courts in it' according to John Stacy in 1819, now houses a thriving antiques centre and café. Appropriately, the inscription on the clock face of the tower reads 'Forget me not'.

NORWICH SCHOOL OF ART AND DESIGN
ST GEORGE'S STREET

The Norwich Technical Institute on St George's Street was built in 1899 and is now part of the Norwich School of Art and Design. Above the entrance are the Norwich city arms of lion and castle. Nearby Blackfriars Bridge was designed by John Soane in 1784.

For the purpose of an Enquiry into the Rise, Progress and Present State of Painting, Architecture and Sculpture, with a view to discover and point out the Best Methods of study to attain to Greatest Perfection in these Arts.

'Manifesto' of the Norwich Society of Artists (the origin of the Norwich School of painters), founded on 19 February 1803 by John Crome.

WIG AND PEN
St Martin's Palace Plain

In 1939 Norwich could boast it had 'a pub for every day of the year, a church for every Sunday'. The Wig and Pen on St Martin's Palace Plain, formerly known as the White Lion, dates from the seventeenth century. Next door is the artist John Sell Cotman's house, which also served as a drawing school from 1824 to 1834.

ELM HILL

Many of the houses in Elm Hill are timber-framed and date from the sixteenth century. But by the 1920s the street had become squalid, full of run-down houses, yards and factories. Only the casting vote of the mayor saved the area from slum clearance in 1924, and the houses were subsequently restored to their former glory.

ELM HILL

Ye valiant men of Norfolk,
whom Nelson's deeds inspire,
Remember his example,
and show your patriot fire.
… We'll save our country's
    freedom,
or in her cause we'll die;
Brave Britons, when united,
the world in arms defy.

ELIZABETH BENTLEY
From 'The Briton's Resolution' (song,
August 1803) in *Poems by Elizabeth Bentley
of Norwich*
1821

ELM HILL

The inhabitants being all busie at
their manufactures, dwell in their
garrets at their looms, and in
their combing-shops, so they call
them, twisting-mills, and other
workhouses; almost all the works
they are employ'd in being done
within doors.

DANIEL DEFOE
*A Tour through the Whole Island
of Great Britain*
1724

ELM HILL

I went through queer medieval streets, many paved with cobblestones, all distinguished by a picturesque dowdiness; some Flemish in appearance, full of houses with the big inverted V on the top storey where the hand-looms were housed; and at night beside the river I might have been in the England or the Netherlands of the fourteenth century with the moon falling on huddled roofs, the lamplight moving in slow waters, the dark figures of men and women going through alleyways between the leaning eaves.

H.V. MORTON
In Search of England
1927

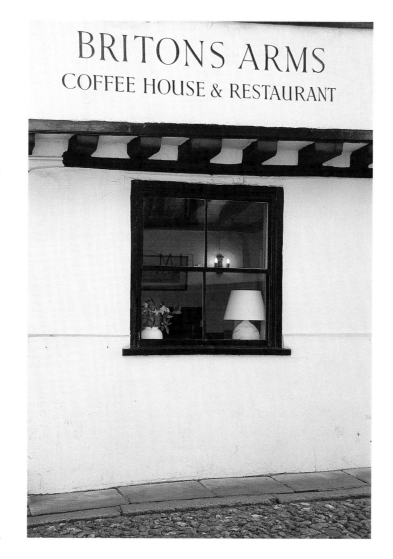

THE BRITON'S ARMS

Now a coffee-house, the Briton's Arms on Elm Street used to be an inn called the King's Head. Its name was changed in 1804, during a time of strong republican feeling. The elm tree from which the street took its name once grew outside.

ST JAMES' MILL

St James' Mill at Whitefriars was built in 1836 on the site of an old Carmelite friary. Originally a yarn mill, it was later used as a box and cracker-making works and, in the interwar period, as a government instructional factory. The building has been owned by Jarrold & Sons Ltd since 1927, and today it houses the company's printing and publishing offices, as well as a number of other organisations.

ST JAMES' MILL

… The Press gives now the final
   stroke, the Weavers to
   supply,
Who work the Yarn into the
   'Piece' of Bombazine to dye,
So thus to finish up my Song,
   I'll give you all a Toast,
'Success to Norwich Trade' we'll
   sing, of which may we long
   boast
In this Noble Norwich Factory,
   one of the present Day.

Verse from 'The Norwich Yarn Factory', sung at St Andrew's Hall on 1 December 1836, the day the mill's foundation stone was laid.

BISHOPSGATE

[Sir Thomas Browne] led me to see all the remarkable places of this ancient Citty, being one of the largest, and certainly after London, one of the noblest of England, for its venerable Cathedrall, number of stately churches, cleanesse of the streetes, and buildings of flints so exquisitely headed and squared as I was much astonished at.

JOHN EVELYN
Diary of John Evelyn
Entry dated 18 October
1671

BISHOPSGATE

This ancient City is pleasantly situated on the Banks of the River Yare, which runs through the midst of it, the Advantage of whose circling streams conduces very much to the Trade and Opulency of this populous City, which is one of the most considerable in Great Britain … At this Time it is reckoned the third City in England for Wealth, Trade, Buildings, and Number of Inhabitants, being exceeded by none but London and Bristol.

JOHN AND JAMES KNAPTON
A Compleat History of the Famous City of Norwich
1728

THE GREAT HOSPITAL
BISHOPSGATE

The Great Hospital was founded by Walter de Suffield, Bishop of Norwich, in October 1249 for needy citizens and 'poor and decrepit chaplains'. The long church was converted into dormitories in the seventeenth century, which accounts for the chimneys in the roof of the nave and chancel.

ADAM AND EVE

The Adam and Eve on Bishopsgate is the oldest pub in Norwich. It was built in 1249 as a brewhouse for cathedral workers and is said to be haunted by Lord Sheffield, who was killed nearby during Kett's Rebellion of 1549. The writer George Borrow was a frequent visitor in the nineteenth century.

BISHOP BRIDGE

Bishop Bridge is the oldest bridge in Norwich, built in about 1340. A fortified gatehouse once stood on the city side. It was due to be demolished in the 1930s but won a last-minute reprieve, and some modern bricks on the parapet date from this time.

NORWICH CATHEDRAL

Whether we look at it from the east or from the west the beauty of its lines thrills us; from the east it rises higher and higher until the eye is drawn as by a magnet to the crowning glory of one of the noblest ancient buildings in the land.

ARTHUR MEE
The King's England: Norfolk
1951

NORWICH CATHEDRAL

… when ['the Swedish Nightingale'] Jenny Lind came to Norwich in 1847 the excitement caused by her visit was intense. During her brief stay, she attended afternoon service in the Cathedral and heard three of the choristers sing the trio, 'Jesus, Heavenly Master,' from Spohr's 'Crucifixation,' with a justness of expression that moved her to tears.

HERBERT LEEDS
Norwich Cathedral Past and Present
1910

NORWICH CATHEDRAL

The length and height of the cathedral nave, emphasised by the perspective of the roof vaulting and the Romanesque arcading from floor level to clerestory, make a dramatic impact on visitors entering from the west front.

NORWICH CATHEDRAL

The interior is at its most powerful when one first sits down in the nave … the styles contributing are the Norman and the Perpendicular, but both speak the same language … Rarely does the unity of English medieval architecture from the eleventh century to the sixteenth century carry so much conviction.

Nikolaus Pevsner and Bill Wilson
The Buildings of England: Norfolk 1, Norwich and North-East
1962

NORWICH CATHEDRAL
CLOISTERS

The Norwich Cloisters form one of the largest and most beautiful quadrangles of the kind in England. The bosses on the eastern side mostly represent foliage, but among them are also to be found sculptures of Four Evangelists, the Scourging, the carrying of the Cross, the Crucifixion, the Resurrection of our Lord, and a quaint figure of Nebuchadnezzar eating grass.

HERBERT LEEDS
Norwich Cathedral Past and Present
1910

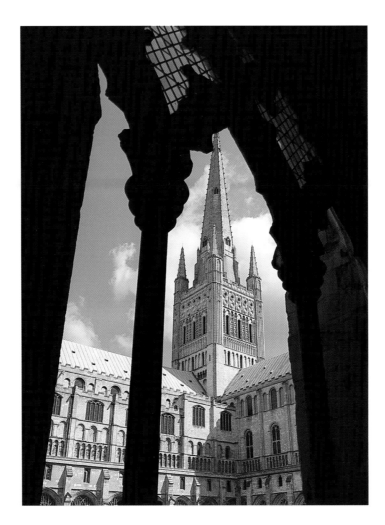

NORWICH CATHEDRAL
CLOISTERS

The heraldic arms of families associated with Queen Elizabeth's visit to Norwich in 1578 can be seen in the windows in north wall of the cloisters.

NORWICH CATHEDRAL CLOISTERS

The construction of the cloisters as we see them today took more than 100 years, from 1297 to 1430, and the Gothic tracery illustrates the developing architectural styles of fourteenth-century England.

NORWICH CATHEDRAL CLOSE

The thermometer fell to zero at Norwich. The cold was so intense that fowls under cover were frozen to death. Great distress prevailed, and meetings were held … to adopt measures for the relief of the poor.

7 January 1841
Norfolk Annals, Vol. 1: a chronological record of remarkable events in the nineteenth century
1901

NORWICH CATHEDRAL
Close

The note of the cuckoo, though uniform, always gives pleasure, because it reminds us that summer is coming. But that pleasure is mixed with melancholy, because we reflect, that what is coming will soon be going again. That is the consideration which embitters every sublunary enjoyment! Let the delight of my heart then be in thee, O Lord and Creator of all things, with whom alone is no variableness, neither show of changing!

GEORGE HORNE
Memoirs of the Reverend George Horne, Bishop of Norwich
1795

NORWICH CATHEDRAL
Close

The layout of the Close is as the Normans left it and the Reformation has hardly altered it, except that after 1538 more townspeople rented houses even if an address in the Close became fashionable only at the end of the seventeenth century. The population rose from 650 in 1693 to 700 in 1752.

NIKOLAUS PEVSNER AND BILL WILSON
The Buildings of England: Norfolk 1, Norwich and North-East
1962

NORWICH SCHOOL

The range of buildings to the north of the Erpingham Gate includes the Carnary Chapel, which was bought by Norwich Corporation in 1547 to house the King Edward VI School. All of these buildings, and several others in the Close, are now used by Norwich School. Admiral Lord Nelson is one of the school's famous 'old boys' and is commemorated by a statue near the west front of the cathedral.

NORWICH CATHEDRAL
RIVERSIDE WALK

The suburbs are large, the prospects sweet, with other amenities, not omitting the flower gardens, in which all the inhabitants excel.

JOHN EVELYN
Diary of John Evelyn
Entry dated 18 October
1671

PULL'S FERRY

Picturesque Pull's Ferry is an ancient water gate on the site of a former canal, built to transport stone during the construction of the cathedral. It is named after James Pull, who operated the ferry across the Wensum to the Close here for forty-five years until his death in 1841. The last ferry crossed in the 1940s.

COW TOWER

Situated on a bend on the River Wensum, Cow Tower was originally a river tollhouse, but by 1378 it was in ruins. It was rebuilt in 1399 – one of the country's first brick buildings – to strengthen the city's defences. Later it was used as a shelter for cattle grazing on nearby meadows.

ST ANDREW'S HALL

This should really be listed as a church; for it was the Dominican or Blackfriars' church of Norwich, and its survival is extremely valuable, as it is the only English friars' church which has come down to our day so complete … the building in its present form dates from 1440–70, rebuilt after a fire, but probably following the early 14th-century plan.

NIKOLAUS PEVSNER AND BILL WILSON
The Buildings of England: Norfolk 1, Norwich and North-East
1962

ST ANDREW'S HALL CRYPT

The old church crypt is now a popular tearoom and meeting-place for visitors to the regular antique fairs, craft markets, flea markets and specialist sales, auctions and exhibitions held in St Andrew's Hall.

ST ANDREW'S HALL
CLOISTERS

The south side of the cloisters is all that remains of the original quadrangle around which the friars would have studied and meditated.

ST ANDREW'S AND BLACKFRIARS' HALLS

St Andrew's and Blackfriars' halls represent the most complete surviving medieval friary buildings in Europe. In 1540, after the Reformation, the city council bought the property from the Duke of Norfolk for £81. Mayor Augustine Steward proposed to 'make the church a fayer and large halle, well pathed, for the mayor and his bretherne, … for their common assemblyes.'

ST ANDREW'S HALL

The church, now the common hall, was begun building in 1415, by the famous Sir Thomas Erpingham … it is a beautiful uniform structure, consisting of a nave of 124 feet long, and 35 broad … its lofty roof is supported by twelve slender pillars.

JOHN STACY
A Topographical and Historical Account of the City and County of Norwich
1819

ST ANDREW'S HALL CRYPT

Bill of Fare (to serve 900)
27 Haunches of Roast Beef
27 of boiled Roast Beef
27 Giblet & Beef Pies
24 Haunches of Roast Mutton
24 Legs of boiled Roast
    Mutton
32 Legs of Roast Pork
125 Plum Puddings
1,000 1d. Loaves
5 Barrels of London Porter
6 Barrels of Norwich Ale

Dinner at St Andrew's Hall, on the occasion of the founding of St James' Yarn Mill in 1836.

EXCHANGE STREET

As I became older, I became more and more unconsciously in love with those gabled houses in their narrow streets. Such an unlimited wealth of motifs would tempt the dullest painter.

Sir Alfred Munnings
An Artist's Life
1950

POTTERGATE

An eminent weaver of Norwich gave me a scheme of their trade on this occasion, by which, calculating from the number of looms at that time employ'd in the city of Norwich only … that there were 120,000 people employ'd in the woollen and silk and wool manufactures.

Daniel Defoe
A Tour through the Whole Island of Great Britain
1724

TIMBER HILL

The front parlour is an almost universal cult in Norwich, jealously preserved for the sole use and enjoyment of the family Bible and the stuffed birds and miscellaneous crockery without which no man be respectable … By day the family overcrowd the one small kitchen, and by night the two or three tiny bedrooms, one of which is very likely partly tenanted by canaries.

C.B. HAWKINS
Norwich – A Social Study
1910

MADDERMARKET THEATRE
Named after the market where dyestuffs were sold in medieval times, the Maddermarket Theatre was formerly a Roman Catholic chapel and was converted into an 'Elizabethan playhouse' by Nugent Monck in 1921.

NORWICH UNION
SENTINEL HOUSE

At the Guildhall in 1792, Thomas Bignold founded the business that was to become Norwich Union. Today it is an international company offering a range of financial services. Sentinel House, pictured here, opened in 1990.

NORWICH UNION
BIGNOLD STATUE

Never perhaps in the history of Norwich, was there such a sight. The spectacle was of a kind that would have done no dishonour to departed Royalty, and testified beyond cavil to the deep-rooted esteem and respect in which the venerable knight was held by all classes in his native city.

Account in *Norfolk Herald* of the funeral in 1875 of Samuel Bignold (son of Thomas), Secretary of the Norwich Union

NORWICH UNION
SURREY HOUSE

The marble used in the main hall of Surrey House had been ordered for Westminster Cathedral, but a strike at the Italian mine delayed delivery. The directors of the Life Society later bought it for £6,000, a phenomenal sum at the time, and the entire building cost £36,000 – the equivalent of more than £12 million today.

NORWICH UNION
SURREY HOUSE

The first dedicated headquarters of the Norwich Union Life Society was intended from the beginning to send a clear and confident message to Norwich and to the wider world in which Norwich Union was becoming internationally known. Reflecting the confidence of the times in British architecture and the decorative arts, it incorporated the neo-classical values of the Italian-inspired English Renaissance and the new 20th-century preoccupations with art nouveau, the Orient, mysticism and romance.

JONATHAN MANTLE
Norwich Union: The First 200 Years
1997

CHAPELFIELD GARDENS

With another youthful friend I would, for the sum of sixpence, enter and stroll around what was then known as Chapel Field Gardens, when on Thursday nights a band played and pretty shop-girls walked in twos or threes in charming dresses. They never even regarded me, shy as a colt, as they passed under the large trees, all lit with coloured lights.

SIR ALFRED MUNNINGS
An Artist's Life
1950

CHAPEL FIELD NORTH

This attractive row of Georgian houses on Chapel Field North overlooks Chapelfield Gardens. Sir John Harrison Yallop, Mayor of Norwich in 1815 and 1831, lived in the balconied house on the left.

CHAPELFIELD GARDENS

The bandstand at Chapelfield Gardens dates from the 1890s and is dedicated to the memory of bandleader Glenn Miller, who played here in 1944.

CATHEDRAL CHURCH OF ST JOHN THE BAPTIST

An amazing church, proof of Victorian generosity and optimism.

NIKOLAUS PEVSNER AND BILL WILSON
The Buildings of England: Norfolk 1, Norwich and North-East
1962

CATHEDRAL CHURCH OF ST JOHN THE BAPTIST

The Cathedral Church of St John the Baptist is the Roman Catholic cathedral and stands on one of the highest points in the city. It was built by George Gilbert Scott and his brother John Oldrid Scott. Opened in 1910, it is a fine example of Victorian ecclesiastical architecture in the Early English Gothic style.

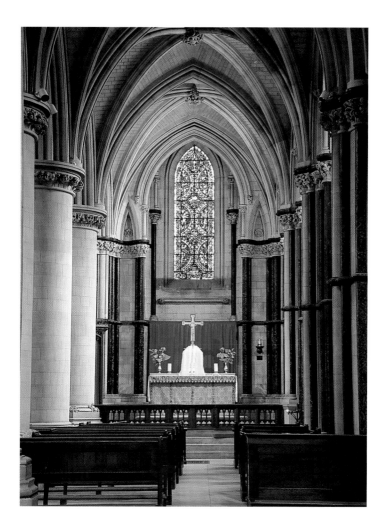

CATHEDRAL CHURCH OF ST JOHN THE BAPTIST

Henry Fitzalan Howard, 15th Duke of Norfolk, paid for much of the work on the church. He donated £20,000 in thanks to God for a happy marriage. Constructed of English limestone, the cathedral contains some of the most beautiful Victorian stained-glass windows in Europe.

CATHEDRAL CHURCH OF ST JOHN THE BAPTIST

After this he treated my soul to a supreme and spiritual pleasure. I was filled with an eternal assurance, which was powerfully maintained, without the least sort of grievous fear. This experience was so happy spiritually that I felt completely at peace and relaxed: nothing on earth could have disturbed me.

JULIAN OF NORWICH
Revelations of Divine Love
1373

OCTAGON CHAPEL
COLEGATE

I was shown Dr Taylor's new meeting house, perhaps the most elegant one in Europe. It is eight-square, built of the finest brick, with sixteen sash-windows below, as many above, and eight skylights in the dome, which, indeed, are purely ornamental. The inside is finished in the highest taste and is as clean as any nobleman's saloon. The communion table is fine mahogany; the very latches of the pew doors are polished brass. How can it be thought that the old, coarse gospel should find admission here?

JOHN WESLEY
Entry from his Journal
1757

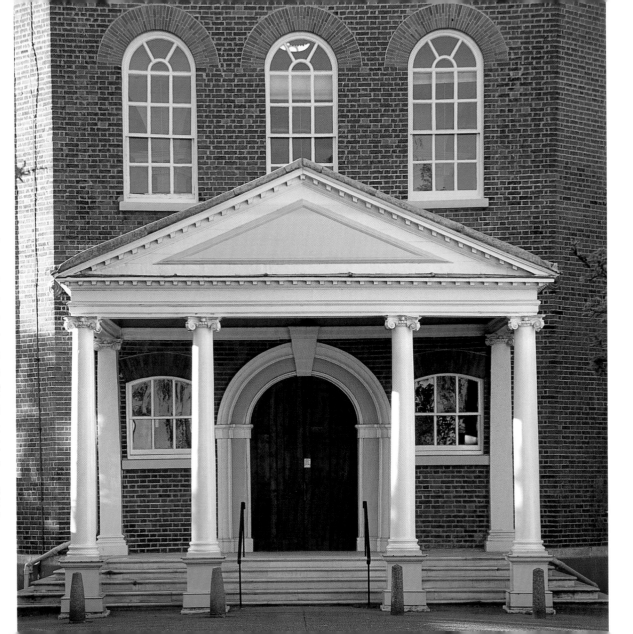

COLEGATE

There are in this city thirty-two parishes besides the cathedral, and a great many meeting-houses of Dissenters of all denominations.

DANIEL DEFOE
A Tour through the Whole Island of Great Britain
1724

ST GEORGE'S
COLEGATE

The interior [of St George's, Colegate] is exciting and different, for the church is fortunate in having retained a good deal of Georgian woodwork, which takes its place so happily in this Gothic fabric.

NOEL SPENCER AND ARNOLD KENT
The Old Churches of Norwich
1970

MOUSEHOLD HEATH

The eye beholds a scene which cannot fail to awaken, even in the least sensitive bosom, feelings of pleasure and admiration. At the foot of the heights flows a narrow and deep river, with an antique bridge communicating with a long and narrow suburb, flanked on either side by rich meadows of the brightest green beyond which spreads the city; the fine old city, perhaps the most curious specimen at present extant of the genuine old English town.

GEORGE BORROW
Lavengro: the Scholar, the Gypsy, the Priest
1851

DRAGON HALL

The old Dragon was yearly the central figure of a huge pageant of St George and the monster, and in that capacity the latter was encountered and vanquished in the most sanguinary manner by the titular saint of the Gild.

W.H. JONES
Bygone Norfolk
1898

Preserved high up in the beams of Dragon Hall's crown-post roof is a superbly carved dragon.

DRAGON HALL

During the restoration of buildings on King Street in the 1980s, a great hall dating from the mid-fifteenth century was discovered. It was apparently once the showroom of a wealthy cloth-merchant. It is now open to the public as Dragon Hall.

ST JULIAN'S CHURCH

In 1373, after receiving the last rites during an illness, Julian of Norwich experienced a series of visions. *Revelations of Divine Love* is an account of the sixteen 'shewings' and her interpretation of these mystical experiences. It is the first known book in English written by an English woman. St Julian's Church, between Rouen Road and King Street, was the site of her cell and contains her shrine.

ST JULIAN'S CHURCH

All this blessed teaching of
our Lord was shown in three
ways: by physical sight, by
words formed in my intellect,
and by spiritual sight …
I had, in some measure, both
touch, sight, and feeling of
three of God's attributes, and
on them the strength and
effectiveness of the whole
revelation depends …
The attributes are these:
life, love and light.

JULIAN OF NORWICH
Revelations of Divine Love
1373

ST JULIAN'S CHURCH

The tiny church of St Julian
was almost entirely rebuilt
after it was bombed in
World War II. Only a stump
remains of the pre-Conquest
tower, and some round
Saxon windows can still be
seen in the nave.

CITY WALLS

The walls of this city are reckon'd three miles in circumference, taking in more ground than the City of London; but much of that ground lying open in pasture-fields and gardens. … The walls seem to be placed, as if they expected that the city would in time encrease sufficiently to fill them up with buildings.

DANIEL DEFOE
A Tour through the Whole Island of Great Britain
1724

THE BLACK TOWER

The Citty … is walled round full of towers, except on the river side which serves for the wall; they seeme the best in repair of any walled citty I know … the carving and battlements and towers looks well.

CELIA FIENNES
The Illustrated Journeys of Celia Fiennes 1685–c. 1712

The Black Tower was strategically sited to give clear views over the southern approaches to the city. It was later used as a prison and as an isolation house for plague victims.

WHITLINGHAM LANE

Here too each city youth and sprightly lass,

In the gay sailing boats are seen to pass,

Adown sweet Wensum's stream on pleasure's wing,

Making with joy the fruitful vale to ring,

Wafted by gentle gales they skim along,

To Whitlingham, to join the festive throng!

JAMES LAMB
From *A Visit to Norwich*
1820

O Summer! hither bend thy cheerful way,

Our clime will gladly hail thy sway;

O! come in all they flowering pride,

With rural Pleasure dancing at thy side.

ELIZABETH BENTLEY
From 'Ode to Summer' in *Poems by Elizabeth Bentley of Norwich*
1821

WHITLINGHAM LITTLE BROAD

Hail! hour of Peace! the happy time,
To meditate on themes sublime;
In union with the tranquil scene,
The mind is sooth'd to thoughts
    serene;
The soul now feeds her heavenly
    birth,
Disdains the trivial joys on earth,
And pants to gain her promised rest,
'Mid the pure spirits of the blest.

ELIZABETH BENTLEY
From 'The Hour of Peace' in *Poems*
by Elizabeth Bentley of Norwich
1821

Whitlingham Little Broad, near
Trowse, is an oasis of calm near the
city, popular with watersports
enthusiasts in the summer months.

TROWSE

There is evidence of
occupation of the Norwich
area from prehistoric times.
Flint tools from the
Mesolithic period and
pottery from the Iron Age
have been found in the valley
of the River Yare at Trowse,
to the south-east of the city.

THORPE RAILWAY STATION

Upon Thursday night,
  in darkness and gloom,
Both trains were rushing, alas !
  to their doom;
The night mail from Yarmouth,
  and the Norwich fast train,
On the same line of rails they
  must meet it was plain.
Over the rails like lightning
  they dash,
Until they both meet with a
  terrible crash,
Nineteen of the passengers
  at that fatal time,
Were mangl'd and crush'd and
  lay dead on the line.

'The Great Eastern Accident near Norwich',
10 September 1874

THORPE RAILWAY STATION

The railway arrived in Norwich
in 1844 from Great Yarmouth,
hence the position of Thorpe
Station on the east side of
the city. Norwich had three
stations at one time, but only
Thorpe Station remains today.
The Grade II-listed building
has now been restored to its
former glory, including the
replacement of the main
roof with zinc fish-tail tiles.

Norwich Station

NORWICH CITY FOOTBALL CLUB

The canary was once the Norwich weaver's companion – now it is the mascot of Norwich City Football Club, formed in June 1902 and one of the oldest football clubs in the world.

Norwich City played its first football league game on 28 August 1920. The highest-ever attendance at the ground was 43,984, when the team played Leicester City in the sixth round of the FA Cup on 30 March 1963. Today, the all-seated ground capacity is 21,414.

RIVERSIDE

A former industrial site with river frontage near Thorpe Railway Station has been developed to create a leisure and amenity area covering 450,000 sq feet (42,000 sq m). The Riverside complex contains a multiscreen cinema, bowling alley, nightclub, bars and restaurants.

RIVERSIDE

Entering Norwich by boat is one of Broadland's most fascinating adventures … Ocean-going cargo boats up to 600 tons laden … discharging their cargoes to the accompaniment of shouts and welcomes in many languages – there is the thrill of navigating in a real port.

What to do on the Norfolk Broads
1958

RIVERSIDE WALK

I saw, with pleasure and surprise,
The beauteous tow'rs of Norwich …
No situation can it surpass in any
    nation,
Neither too low, nor yet too high,
Not over-moist, nor over dry:
Inclining to the morning ray;
By pleasant views and villas bounded,
Dry sheltr'ing hills and woods
    surrounded,
Above, a wide expanse of fields
A pure and constant fragrance yields;
Below, two silver streamlets meet,
And lay their tribute at its feet.

ALEXANDER GEDDES
A Norfolk Tale – a Journal from London to Norwich
1742

THORPE WAR MEMORIAL

In one warm glow of christian love
Forgot all proud distinctions seem;
The rich, the poor, together rove;
Their eyes with answering kindness beam.

Blest sound! Blest sight! … but pray ye pause
And bid my eager wonder cease;
Of joy like this, say what's the cause?
A thousand voices answer … 'PEACE!'

AMELIA OPIE   From 'Lines written at Norwich on the first news of peace' in *Poems* 1806

UNIVERSITY OF EAST ANGLIA

The room is raw in the wet, dull light; it is a simple rectangle, with unpainted breeze-block walls, described in the architectural journals as proof of Kaakinen's frank honesty. The rooms at Watermouth are all like this, stark, simple, repetitious, each one an exemplary instance of all the others … beyond the windows you can see, dead centre, the high phallus, eolipilic in shape, of the boilerhouse chimney, the absolute focus, the point of maximum architectural eminence, of the entire university, its substitute for a tower or spire or campanile.

MALCOLM BRADBURY
The History Man
1975

The fictional University of Watermouth was based on the new British universities of the 1960s, including UEA, where Sir Malcolm Bradbury taught from 1965 to 1995.

UNIVERSITY OF EAST ANGLIA

The University of East Anglia admitted its first eighty-seven undergraduates in 1963. The pyramidal student-residences of Norfolk and Suffolk terraces, which architect Denys Lasdun called Ziggurats after the temples of ancient Mesopotamia, form a striking backdrop to the man-made University Broad.

Lasdun's original intention, that no building on campus should be more than five minutes' walk from any other, has largely been honoured despite building expansion in the last decade.

UNIVERSITY OF EAST ANGLIA

Graceful reclining figures by Sir Henry Moore complement the Sainsbury Centre for Visual Arts, a masterpiece of modern gallery design.

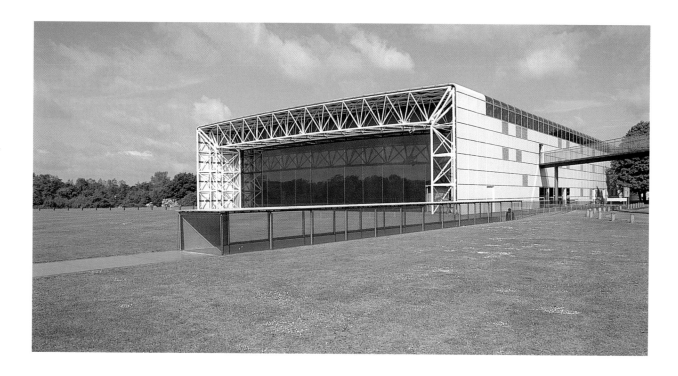

THE SAINSBURY CENTRE FOR VISUAL ARTS

Simplicity is the key … the beauty of [Foster's] buildings relies on precise engineering computations presented in the vocabulary of machinery.

Nikolaus Pevsner and Bill Wilson
The Buildings of England: Norfolk 1, Norwich and North-East
1962

UNIVERSITY OF EAST ANGLIA

Students' living and teaching facilities were very closely associated indeed, a Utopian ideal reflecting the spirit of free universal education and the notion that all students are dedicated to nothing but study. The architects, for instance, felt that the walkways would stimulate interdisciplinary exchanges as students passed and mingled.

NIKOLAUS PEVSNER AND BILL WILSON
*The Buildings of England: Norfolk 1,
Norwich and North-East*
1962

The stag on Orford Hill, formerly of Darlow & Company, gunmakers

Acknowledgements

Every effort has been made to secure permissions from copyright owners to use the extracts of text featured in this book. Any subsequent correspondence should be sent to Jarrold Publishing at the following address: Jarrold Publishing, Whitefriars, Norwich NR3 1TR.

page

13 (top left) *The Norfolk Tour or Traveller's Pocket-Companion* by R. Beatniffe. R. Beatniffe, 1773.

13 (bottom left) *The Buildings of England: Norfolk 1, Norwich and North-East* by Nikolaus Pevsner and Bill Wilson. Penguin Books, 1992; second edition 1997. Reproduced by permission of Penguin Books Ltd.

13 (right) *People of Medieval Norwich* by Charles B. Jewson. Jarrold, 1951.

14 *Three Centuries of a City Library* by George A. Stephen. Public Library Committee (Norwich), 1917.

17 As for page 13 (bottom left).

19 (left) *The Illustrated Journeys of Celia Fiennes 1685-c. 1712*, ed. by Christopher Morris. Webb & Bower (Publishers) Ltd, 1982.

19 (right) *Castle Meadow: a story of Norwich a hundred years ago* by Emma Marshall. Seeley & Co, 1899.

20 *Citizens of No Mean City*. Jarrold, 1910.

23 (left) *Norwich – A Social Study* by C.B. Hawkins. Philip Lee Warner, 1910.

23 (right) *John Wesley's Journal* (Spiritual Lives series), abbreviated by Percy Livingstone Parker, ed. by Robert Blackhouse. Hodder & Stoughton, 1993. Reproduced by permission of Hodder & Stoughton Ltd.

24 *Souvenir of a visit to Carrow Works, Norwich*. J. & J. Colman Ltd, 1901. By kind permission of Colman's.

28 *The Norfolk Road: An East Anglian Highway* by Charles G. Harper. Chapman & Hall, 1901.

31 As for page 19 (right).

32 *A Tour through the Whole Island of Great Britain* by Daniel Defoe (1724), ed. by P.N. Furbank, W.R. Owens & A.I. Coulson. Yale University Press, 1991.

35 As for page 20.

36 As for page 19 (left).

42 (left) *Poems by Elizabeth Bentley of Norwich*. Stevenson, Matchett & Stevenson, 1821.

42 (right) As for page 32.

45 *In Search of England* by H.V. Morton. Methuen Publishing Ltd, 1927.

46 Quoted in *St James' Mill* (pamphlet) by P.S. Salt. Jarrold, 1996.

49 (left) *Diary of John Evelyn*, ed. by E.S. de Beer. OUP, 1959. By permission of Oxford University Press.

49 (right) *A Compleat History of the Famous City of Norwich*. John and James Knapton, 1728.

53 *The King's England: Norfolk* by Arthur Mee. © The estate of Arthur Mee and The King's England Press Ltd.

55 *Norwich Cathedral Past and Present* by Herbert Leeds. H. J. Vince, 1910.

57 As for page 13 (bottom left).

58 As for page 55.

61 *Norfolk Annals, Vol. 1: a chronological record of remarkable events in the nineteenth century*, ed. by Charles Mackie. Norfolk Chronicle, 1901.

62 (left) *Memoirs of the Reverend George Horne, Bishop of Norwich*, ed. by W. Jones. G.C. & J. Robinson et al., 1795.

62 (right) As for page 13 (bottom left).

65 As for page 49 (left).

69 As for page 13 (bottom left)

73 (left) *A Topographical and Historical Account of the City and County of Norwich* by John Stacy. Longman, Hurst, Rees, Orme & Brown, 1819.

73 (right) As for page 46.

74 (top) *An Artist's Life* by Sir Alfred Munnings. Museum Press, 1950.

74 (bottom) As for page 32.

77 As for page 23 (left).

78 *Norwich Union: The First 200 Years* by Jonathan Mantle. © Norwich Union. James & James, 1997.

80 As for page 78.

83 As for page 74 (top).

84 As for page 13 (bottom left).

88 *Revelations of Divine Love* by Julian of Norwich (1373), translated by Clifton Wolters. Penguin Classics, 1966. Reproduced by kind permission of John Wolters.

90 As for page 23 (right).

91 (left) As for page 32.

91 (right) *The Old Churches of Norwich* by Noel Spencer and Arnold Kent. Jarrold, 1970.

93 *Lavengro: the Scholar, the Gypsy, the Priest* by George Borrow. Humphrey Milford/OUP, 1851.

95 *Bygone Norfolk*, ed. by William Andrews. William Andrews & Co, 1898.

98 As for page 88.

101 (left) As for page 32.

101 (right) As for page 19 (left).

102 (top) *A Visit to Norwich* by James Lamb. N. Stewardson, 1820.

102 (bottom) As for page 42 (left).

105 As for page 42 (left).

110 *What to do on the Norfolk Broads*. Jarrold, 1958.

113 (left) *A Norfolk Tale – a Journal from London to Norwich* by Alexander Geddes. Norwich, 1742.

113 (right) *Poems* by Amelia Opie. Longman, Hurst, Rees & Orme, 1806.

114 *The History Man* by Malcolm Bradbury. Martin Secker & Warburg, 1975. By kind permission of Curtis Brown Group Ltd. on behalf of © Malcolm Bradbury 1975.

117 As for page 13 (bottom left).

118 As for page 13 (bottom left).

Bibliography

Editions and dates in this bibliography are those of the items that have been examined. In some cases earlier editions have significant differences to those listed here.

Beatniffe, R.: *The Norfolk Tour or Traveller's Pocket-Companion* by R. Beatniffe. R. Beatniffe, 1773.

Bentley, Elizabeth: *Poems by Elizabeth Bentley of Norwich*. Stevenson, Matchett & Stevenson, 1821.

Borrow, George: *Lavengro: the Scholar, the Gypsy, the Priest*. Humphrey Milford/OUP, 1851.

Bradbury, Malcolm: *The History Man*. Martin Secker & Warburg, 1975.

Brooks, J.A.: *Railway Ghosts*. Jarrold Publishing, 1985.

Browne, Philip *A History of Norwich: Bacon*, Kinnebrook, 1814.

Bygone Norfolk, edited by William Andrews. W. Andrews & Co, 1898.

Citizens of No Mean City. Jarrold, 1910.

City of Norwich official guide. Jarrold Publishing, 2001.

A Compleat History of the Famous City of Norwich. John and James Knapton, 1728.

Diary of John Evelyn, edited by E.S. de Beer. OUP, 1959.

Dutt, William A.: *Some Literary Associations of East Anglia*. Methuen, 1907.

Fuller, Thomas: *The History of the Worthies of England* (1662). Thomas Tegg, 1840.

Geddes, Alexander: *A Norfolk Tale – a Journal from London to Norwich*. 1742.

Harper, Charles G.: *The Norfolk Road: An East Anglian Highway*. Chapman & Hall, 1901.

Hawkins, C.B.: *Norwich – A Social Study*. Philip Lee Warner, 1910.

H.V. Morton's Britain, edited by Gilbert Carter. Methuen & Co, 1969.

The Illustrated Journeys of Celia Fiennes 1685–c. 1712, edited by Christopher Morris. Webb & Bower, 1982.

Jacobs, Michael and Warner, Malcolm: *Art in East Anglia*. Jarrold, 1980.

Jewson, Charles B.: *People of Medieval Norwich*. Jarrold, 1951.

Julian of Norwich: *Revelations of Divine Love* (1373). Penguin Classics, 1966.

Kent, Arnold and Stephenson, Andrew: *Norwich Inheritance*. Jarrold, 1948.

Lamb, James: *A Visit to Norwich*. N. Stewardson, 1820.

Leeds, Herbert: *Norwich Cathedral Past and Present*. H.J. Vince, 1910.

Mantle, Jonathan: *Norwich Union: The First 200 Years*. James & James, 1997.

Marshall, Emma: *Castle Meadow: a story of Norwich a hundred years ago*. Seeley & Co, 1899.

Mee, Arthur: *The King's England: Norfolk*. Hodder & Stoughton 1951.

Memoirs of the Reverend George Horne, Bishop of Norwich, edited by William Jones. G.C. & J. Robinson *et al.*, 1795.

Munnings, Sir Alfred: *An Artist's Life*. Museum Press, 1950.

Nobbs, George: *Norwich City Hall*. Norwich City Council, 1988.

Norfolk Annals, Vol. 1: a chronological record of remarkable events in the nineteenth century, edited by Charles Mackie. Norfolk Chronicle, 1901

Opie, Amelia: *Poems*. Longman, Hurst, Rees & Orme, 1806.

Pevsner, Nikolaus and Wilson, Bill: *The Buildings of England: Norfolk 1, Norwich and North-East*. First published 1962. Penguin, 1997.

Salt, P.S.: *St James' Mill*. Jarrold (pamphlet), 1996.

Souvenir of a visit to Carrow Works, Norwich. J. & J. Colman Ltd, 1901.

Spencer, Noel and Kent, Arnold. *The Old Churches of Norwich*. Jarrold, 1970.

Stacy, John: *A Topographical and Historical Account of the City and County of Norwich*. Longman, Hurst, Rees, Orme & Brown, 1819.

Stephen, George A.: *Three Centuries of a City Library*. Public Library Committee (Norwich), 1917.

Timpson, John: *Timpson's Towns of England and Wales*. Jarrold, 1989.

A Tour through the Whole Island of Great Britain by Daniel Defoe (1724), edited by P.N. Furbank. W.R. Owens & A.J. Coulson. Yale University Press, 1991.

Wearing, Stanley J.: *Georgian Norwich*. Jarrold, 1926.

Wesley, John: *John Wesley's Journal* (Spiritual Lives series), abbreviated by Percy Livingstone Parker, edited by Robert Blackhouse. Hodder & Stoughton, 1993.

What to do on the Norfolk Broads. Jarrold, 1958.

Hook's Walk, Cathedral Close

St John Maddermarket, Pottergate

Index

GROUNDCOVER
SERIES